SOCCER

BY JACK SCAGNETTI

HARVEY HOUSE · PUBLISHERS · NEW YORK

ACKNOWLEDGMENTS

Special thanks to Sandy Weinstock and Earl Needham, Regional Commissioners, San Fernando Valley area, for American Youth Soccer Organization; players of the AYSO for demonstrative technique photographs, and to the United States Soccer Federation.

Harvey House, Publishers
20 Waterside Plaza, New York, New York 10010

Published in Canada by Fitzhenry & Whiteside, Ltd., Toronto

CONTENTS

CHAPTER ONE ● HISTORY

No sport enjoys as much world-wide popularity as soccer. It is played in 140 countries by more than 250 million registered players before nearly 675 million spectators. It is called football in all countries except the United States and Canada where the name of the game is soccer.

Although its origins can be traced to ancient Rome, Greece, China and Egypt, the modern version of soccer dates back to 1863 when the London Football Association was formed in England. The Association adopted the first set of unified rules which were written a year earlier. Soccer soon spread to other countries. Professional leagues were organized and inter-country matches became popular. Today professional soccer stars are paid large salaries and are international heroes. Soccer stadiums are jampacked with enthusiastic spectators. Crowds of 100,000 are not uncommon in many countries.

Youngsters can begin playing soccer at a very early age. In many countries children can be seen kicking a soccer ball on the streets and in playgrounds.

Pele (Edson Arantes do Nasciemento), generally recognized as the greatest soccer player of all time, began playing at the age of five and he joined a professional team in Brazil at age 15. Wherever he played, he drew huge crowds and when he joined the New York Cosmos of the North American Soccer League in 1975 he helped further enthusiasm for soccer in the U.S.A., where the sport has been growing since the mid-1950's. Pele became the world's highest paid athlete—he received $4.75 million for a three-year contract. He retired from league competition at age 36 in October, 1977, after a 22-year professional career in which he played in 65 countries.

Compared with other sports, soccer has been slow to gain popularity in the United States although the game has been played here for over 100 years. But since the late 1960's soccer's growth in the U.S.A. has been phenomenal. Today nearly 700 colleges and universities participate in intercollegiate soccer while nearly 3,000 high schools play interscholastic soccer. The number is expected to increase dramatically because rising costs of football equipment and liability insurance will cause many colleges and schools to replace football with soccer, which is a far less dangerous and less expensive sport.

Paralleling the growth of professional soccer leagues in the U.S.A., which now draw huge crowds, is the boom soccer is experiencing among America's young people. More and more boys and girls are discovering the sport and competing in youth soccer leagues. For example, the American Youth Soccer League, only one of many organizations promoting soccer, has grown from nine teams in one age division in 1964 to more than 8,500 teams and 830,000 players registered nationwide. Parents who have never seen a game prior to their children's participation are becoming real soccer enthusiasts.

Soccer is governed throughout the world by the Federation Internationale de Football Association, commonly called FIFA. In the United States soccer activity is sanctioned and promoted by the United States Soccer Federation, commonly called USSF. In July, 1974, the USSF approved the constitution of the new United States Youth Soccer Federation, the USYSA, whose purpose is "to develop, promote and administer the game of soccer among players under 19 years of age." State Youth Associations, consisting of annually affiliated local leagues and/or teams, select their own playing season depending upon, among other things, the weather and availability of playing fields.

There are many factors that make soccer an appealing sport. It is an inexpensive team sport, since the ball is the only essential item of equipment and the game can be played in any open field. Soccer can be taught indoors and out. Players have an equal chance regardless of their height and weight. The rules and strategy of the game are easily understood. Because speed and endurance are vital to success, it promotes physical fitness. Development of individual and team strategy requires mental alertness, and the sport promotes cooperation and teamwork. Chances of injuries are relatively small, and injuries are usually only of a minor nature. The continuous movement, featuring a great amount of running, team play and wide-open action makes it not only exciting for players but for spectators as well. Soccer is one of the few team sports that can be played from age 5 to 50. Because international rules prevail in soccer, language and social barriers are easily overcome and the sport can serve to foster goodwill between nations.

Soccer, which easily accommodates large groups in an organized recreational activity, is an ideal fun-and-fitness sport for any physical education program or for just plain fun after school or on the weekends.

9

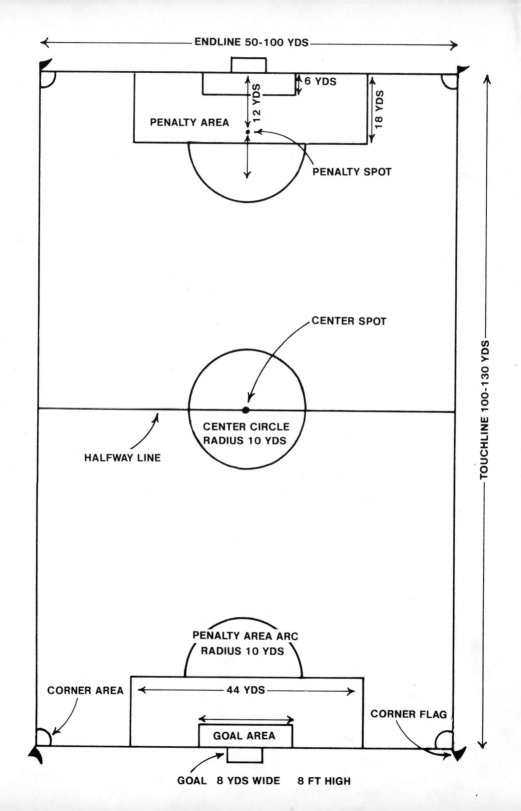

ENDLINE 50-100 YDS

6 YDS

12 YDS

18 YDS

PENALTY AREA

PENALTY SPOT

TOUCHLINE 100-130 YDS

CENTER SPOT

CENTER CIRCLE
RADIUS 10 YDS

HALFWAY LINE

PENALTY AREA ARC
RADIUS 10 YDS

44 YDS

CORNER AREA

CORNER FLAG

GOAL AREA

GOAL   8 YDS WIDE   8 FT HIGH

CHAPTER TWO ● THE FIELD AND EQUIPMENT

Any large grassy area can be marked off for a soccer field. A football field, for example, can be easily converted into a soccer field by using portable soccer goals placed in front of existing goal posts. Keep in mind the overall size of a soccer field should be no more than 130 yards nor less than 100 yards long and no more than 100 yards nor less than 50 yards wide. The standard width for international games is 65 yards.

While smaller fields are recommended for players under the age of 12 (never less than 40 by 80 yards), a standard field should measure 120 yards long and 75 yards wide. A soccer field, like a football field, should always be longer than it is wide.

The field is marked with an outside boundary. The lines along the length of the field are the touchlines, the lines running across at the ends of the field are the goal lines. Corner flags mark each corner of the field. A halfway (midfield) line cuts the field of play into two equal parts. The center of the field should be marked and have a circle with a 10-yard radius around it.

Each end has a goal area which extends six yards into the field from the goal line and is 20 yards wide. A penalty area encloses the goal area. It extends 18 yards from the goal area and is 44 yards wide. A penalty mark, two feet in width, is set 12 yards from the goal line at a mid-point in the field. Penalty kicks are made from this line. An arc of a circle with a 10-yard radius is marked outside the penalty area using the penalty mark as its center. Goals are placed on the center of each goal line and consist of two upright posts eight yards apart (inside measurement) joined by a horizontal crossbar. The lower edge of the bar is eight feet above the ground.

All balls used in a game should be of the same make: round and made of leather. No dangerous material should be used in its construction. The circumference of the ball should not be more than 28 inches nor less than 27 inches. Players under 12 may use balls two inches smaller and two ounces lighter. At the start of the game the weight of the ball should not be more than 16 ounces (454.4 grams) nor less than 14 ounces (397.6 grams), and the weight should not exceed 16.75 ounces (475 grams) even when wet and used. The ball should be inflated to a pressure which will require the ball, when dropped from a height of 100 inches to a smooth cement floor, to rebound between 60 and 65 inches.

A number of soccer balls on the market meet these specifications and usually the manufacturer will indicate on the ball the recommended air pressure to meet the above standards. Some balls are waterproof, while others are water-repellent.

It costs considerably less to equip a soccer team than most other major sports. Players wear only a jersey, shorts, knee-length stockings, shin guards, and soccer shoes with cleats of leather, rubber, nylon or light alloys. All cleats, studs or bars, should not be less than one-half inch in diameter or width and should not stick out from the sole or heel of the shoe more than 3/4-inch. A molded shoe with multiple cleats less than one-half inch in diameter should not extend more than 5/16-inch from the sole.

Soccer uniforms should allow for comfort, protection, and easy identification for teammates and spectators.

It is illegal to use any hard or dangerous head, face, or body protection. Kneebraces with metal parts are permissable if no metal is exposed.

Younger players usually wear gym shoes because they are safer and help them to more easily develop the touch essential to control the ball.

Goalkeepers wear specialized gear: pants with thigh pads, knee pads, and gloves that allow for better gripping in cold or wet weather. In addition, goalkeepers wear a jersey that is different in color than both teams to distinguish them from the other players, and often wear a cap to help shield their eyes from the sun.

Numbers on the back of the jerseys are six inches high and worn by all players.

Balls and shoes will last longer if given proper care. A wet ball should be dried at room temperature, and its surface then rubbed with an oil-base leather dressing. Balls should be stored in a cool, dry place. If stored for a long period, the normal air pressure should be reduced by one-half. Shoes should be cleaned after every game or practice session. Wax or oil them occasionally for extra protection.

Soccer's fast-moving action requires on-the-spot decisions and constant attention.

16

CHAPTER THREE ● PLAYING THE GAME

Playing the game of soccer can be a lot of fun. It has enough features of some of the more interesting team sports to make it appealing to those who want vigorous action, yet it is not as dangerous. Soccer is similar to American football only in that it's a game played by two teams of 11 players each who try to get the ball into their opponents' goal. But it is more like basketball or hockey because possession of the ball changes constantly and it features continuous action with drama, speed and excitement.

The ever-changing ball possession leaves little opportunity for set plays, and yet team formations and tactics are a vital part of the game.

Because of the fast moving action you have to make on-the-spot decisions and yet you have the opportunity to be an individual with skills and style all your own. Unlike football, soccer allows no time to consider pre-game strategy or a numbered play. Quick thinking and speed of movement by individual players allow for exciting action and teamwork.

It's a challenging sport because you must learn to maneuver the ball without using your hands and arms. You control and move the ball only with your feet, legs, chest, and any part of the body except your hands and arms. However, goalkeepers are allowed to use their hands and arms.

Soccer is a sport that allows a player to be active from age 6-18 in elementary and high school and then participate in it in inter-collegiate competition and perhaps move on to professional or amateur teams. You can continue playing into the middle years of life.

Soccer offers plenty of exciting action — dribbling past opponents, a well-executed pass, an intricate and deceptive maneuver, and outstanding defensive play, particularly a diving stop by a goalkeeper.

A goal in soccer is scored when the whole of the ball crosses the goal line between the goal post and under the cross bar, but it cannot be carried, thrown or moved by the arm or hand of an attacking player. Each goal counts for one point. The team scoring the greatest number of goals during a game is the winner.

The game is played in two equal time periods of 45 minutes each, called halves. The halftime interval is five minutes, but can be longer with the consent of the referee. Junior teams usually reduce the game to 60 minutes of play (two 30-minute halves or four 15-minute quarters). Play is started at the beginning of each period, and after a goal, by a kickoff. The referee tosses a coin to determine the choice of ends and the kickoff at the start of the game.

18

Soccer rules are basically simple and easy to follow. There are 17 rules (called laws) in total and they are designed to keep the game moving and keep stoppages to a minimum.

RULES OF POSSESSION

If the ball goes out of bounds during play, either on the ground or in the air, it is thrown in from the point where it crosses the line by a player opposite the team which last touched it. The thrower uses both hands and delivers the ball from behind and over his head. The thrower is not allowed to play the ball again until it has been touched or played by another player. A goal cannot be scored directly from a throw-in.

When the ball passes over the goal line but doesn't score a goal, it is put back into play beyond the penalty area in that half of the goal area nearest to where it went out of bounds. It is returned to play by a player of the defending team, usually the goalkeeper. If the ball is not kicked beyond the penalty area, directly into play, the kick is retaken.

When the ball goes over the goal line without scoring and was last touched by a defender it is put back into play with a corner kick taken by an attacking player.

VIOLATIONS AND FOULS

Violations of soccer rules are divided into two categories: major fouls, for which the penalty is the awarding of direct free kicks; and minor violations, which are penalized by the awarding of indirect free kicks. In direct free kicks, goals may be scored directly from the kick. In indirect kicks, a goal can be scored only if a second player from either team has touched the ball after the kick has been taken.

There are nine major fouls. Four of them condemn illegal use of the hands and arms — handling the ball, pushing, striking or holding an opponent. Use of the feet are involved in three of the fouls: kicking, tripping, or jumping at an opponent. Two of the fouls are for illegal use of the body: charging into an opponent recklessly, and charging from behind. Soccer rules do allow one form of body contact: shoulder charging, where the player may nudge an opponent away from the ball by making solid shoulder-to-shoulder contact. When shoulder charging you must keep your arms close to your side to avoid illegal use of elbows, and the ball must be within playing distance.

Minor fouls include arguing with the referee, intentionally obstructing an opponent when not playing the ball, shoulder charging when the ball is not within playing distance, offside, reckless play, and when a goalkeeper carries the ball more than four steps without releasing it.

Whenever any of the nine major fouls is committed by the defending team in its own penalty area, the attacking team is awarded a penalty kick. The kick is taken on the penalty spot, 12 yards from the goal. The player of the attacking team shoots at the goal with only the goalkeeper to beat. All other players on both teams must be outside the penalty area and penalty arc. The rules prevent the goalkeeper from use of his feet until the ball has been kicked. The odds, obviously, favor the kicker.

Probably the most commonly misunderstood rule in soccer is the *offside* law. As an attacking player, you are offside if a pass is made to you and you are ahead of the ball. That is, if you are nearer to the opponents' goal line than the ball is. If there are fewer than two defenders between you and their goal line or if you are in the opponents' half of the field without the ball, you are offside as well.

If you are standing in your own half of the field and the ball comes to you after an opponent has touched it or played it, you are not offside. You are not offside when you receive the ball directly from a goal kick, corner kick, throw-in, or when the referee has dropped the ball.

OTHER RULES TO KEEP IN MIND

Any of the other players may change places with the goalkeeper provided the referee is informed before the change is made during a break in the action.

In secondary and prep schools, official National Collegiate Athletic Association (NCAA) rules apply with some exceptions. A rubber-covered ball may be substituted for a leather-covered one if it meets NCAA specifications and is considered legal by your association. Any number of substitutions may be made. The time of the game may vary anywhere from 8- to 15-minute quarters, depending on the age of the players and your league rules. Extra periods may be used to decide a tie game. The recommended size of the field of play is 110 yards by 70 yards maximum for high school, and 100 yards by 65 yards maximum for junior high school.

THE REFEREE AND THE LINESMEN

The referee, assisted by two linesmen, has the final decision in the enforcement of the rules. The linesmen's duties are to indicate when the ball is out of play and which side is entitled to the corner kick, goal kick, or throw-in. They also assist the referee in controlling the game.

The best kicking surfaces are the flat areas of the foot, as indicated by arrows. Soccer players seldom kick with the toe. Maintaining good balance is essential when kicking. Ball should be struck slightly below center. Be sure to follow through.

CHAPTER FOUR • LEARNING BASIC SKILLS

Soccer is a unique sport in that players (except for goalkeepers) have to learn to control the ball without using their hands. No matter how good an athlete you are, it's going to take a lot of practice and plenty of game experience to acquire the fundamental skills and become a good soccer player. You must learn to control the ball by using your feet, legs, head or body.

There are several basic skills: kicking, passing, dribbling, trapping, heading, tackling (blocking), and throwing-in. Naturally, the better your all-around ability the more valuable you will be to your team. You can't specialize in one or two skills and be an effective player. You must acquire all the talents. Fortunately, none of the skills require that you be tall or muscular. Most good soccer players have average physiques.

Since soccer is a game of continuous movement, it demands that you always be on the alert and ready to move quickly in any direction, keeping your eye on the ball at all times. Soccer's emphasis on running and use of the feet means that you must be in good physical condition.

KICKING

The most important factor in kicking is accuracy. You should learn to kick equally well with both your right and left foot. There are several different kinds of kicks, but each demands that you keep your head down and your eyes on the ball and allow your leg to follow through after striking the ball.

Soccer players seldom kick straight-on with their toe like football kickers do. The game's most fundamental kick is the instep kick, where the toe is pointing down. The instep, which is the arched upper part of the foot underneath the lacing of the shoe, permits you to place a wide surface of your foot in contact with the ball. This promotes power, accuracy and distance.

In making the kick, swing your kicking leg forward, keeping your toes pointed down and your knee bent, and then straighten the leg as you kick through. The ball should be struck slightly below center.

There are two types of instep kicks: a lofted one and a low drive. For a lofted shot, place your non-kicking foot to the side of the ball and slightly behind it. Make contact with your kicking foot slightly below the center of the ball, enabling your instep to lift the ball. Take a full backswing with the kicking leg, keeping the knee almost fully bent.

The low shot is used most often because it travels with greater speed. For a low shot, place the standing foot alongside the ball and lean your body forward enough so that at impact the knee of your kicking foot is directly over or slightly in front of the ball. The toes of the kicking foot are pointed more downward than with the lofted kick. The knee is straightened as the kick is made and there is a full follow through.

Another often used kick is the inside-of-the-foot kick. The inside of the foot is the area between the big toe and the point of the anklebone. This kick is especially useful when accuracy is more important than distance, particularly in passes of up to 25 yards, and for dribbling. This kick should not be used when power or distance are essential.

To make an inside-of-the-foot kick, place your non-kicking foot to the side and slightly behind the ball. Swing your kicking foot forward with the knee bent and the knee and foot turned slightly outward. Strike the center of the ball with your foot a couple inches off the ground. Straighten your leg as you kick forward and follow through.

Another widely used kick is the outside-of-the-foot kick. This kick is useful for quick, soft and deceptive passes between players on the run, as the ball can be flicked away at the last moment of a running stride. In making this kick, lift your kicking foot slightly off the ground and tap the ball with the outside area of the foot just behind the small toe. Aim for the center of the ball.

An important kick to master is the lift or chip kick, which is used to get the ball over an opponent's head when the player is five or six yards away. Make contact with the ball using the upper part of your shoe above the toes. Slide your foot under the ball to lift it up and lean your body backward. This is not a very powerful kick.

DRIBBLING

Dribbling, the art of manipulating the ball from one foot to the other while going through and around opponents, is one of the most important and exciting skills. The control of the ball while dribbling is achieved by soft strokes with the inside and outside of the instep. The good dribbler makes deceptive changes in pace and direction to elude and confuse opponents.

In execution of the inside-of-the-foot dribble, your foot is turned slightly out to allow the inside of the instep to come in contact with the ball. **The front part of the foot, closer to the toes, is used in dribbling. Use short strides, push the ball along the inside of your feet, raising the kicking foot an inch or two above the ground.** For an outside-of-the-foot dribble, turn your foot inward pigeon-toe style and stroke the ball softly with the outside of the foot just above the toes using short strides, alternating each foot to propel the ball.

Dribbling requires considerable skill and can only be mastered with plenty of practice. You must learn to keep the ball close to you to maintain possession. You must be able to feint your moves to confuse opponents by use of your legs, hips, and shoulder. Good balance is vital to the art of dribbling. You must have such control over the ball's movement that you can quickly change direction, pace, stop, go or pass. The ball should be kept close to your feet when you dribble at slow speeds. At fast speeds keep the ball two to three feet ahead of you so you can maintain your stride while running. Unlike kicking where the head is kept down and the eyes are on the ball, dribbling necessitates that you control the ball without looking at it as you must be able to see your opponent and observe where the defenders are moving.

VOLLEYING

In a game as many as half of the balls coming to you will be in the air and at different speeds and heights. Anytime you kick the ball while it's still in the air, it's called a volley. How you kick the ball will depend upon the height of the ball, its direction and speed. Most of the time the volley kick is basically the same as the instep kick, except for the height of the kicking leg when the ball is hit.

When a ball comes directly to you in flight and is about knee high, it's best to lean back slightly as you prepare to kick. Keep in mind the further back you lean, the higher the ball will go. Timing is essential in any volley kick. You must get your foot to the ball at the right moment.

The inside-of-the-foot kick is used often in volleys and is good for short and accurate passing of the ball as it gives you the greatest contact surface and control. The inside-of-the-foot is also ideal for clearing long passes in defense.

When you kick the ball just as it rebounds off the ground, it is known as a half volley.

fenders will use the instep volley to clear ball away from al area. Side-foot volley is best for control and accuracy. r low balls point your toes down and hit the ball with the instep.

TRAPPING

When you stop the ball to get it into a position where you can dribble, pass or shoot it, that is called trapping. Any part of the body, except the hands and arms, can be used to trap the ball.

To successfully trap the ball, whether rolling, bouncing or in the air, fast or slow, you must allow your body to cushion the ball upon impact to "give" a little. This will prevent the ball from bouncing away. If you allow your body to crash into a moving ball, the ball will surely bound away. The idea is to trap the ball so it stops dead.

One of the most effective ways of trapping is with the inside of your foot, especially on ground balls. Your trapping foot should be about six inches off the ground, and the lower part of your leg must be leaned slightly over the top of the ball which is stopped with the inside of the foot the moment it strikes the ground. You can also apply an outside-of-the-foot trap using the same method.

There will be times when you can't get into proper position for an inside or outside foot trap, and you will then want to stop the ball as it hits the ground with the sole of your foot, which serves as a wedge against the ball and the ground. Your ankle joint must be relaxed. Bear in mind that a foot trap, which stops the action momentarily, doesn't allow you to get the ball moving as fast as the inside or outside foot trap.

When a dropping ball comes toward you just below your waist you can trap the ball with your thigh. Raise your leg with your knee bent, allowing the ball to strike the middle and inside part of the thigh just above the kneecap. You can cushion the ball by lowering your thigh slightly at the exact moment of contact. This causes the ball to drop to the ground.

If a ball comes toward you higher than the waist and lower than the neck, you should trap it with your chest. If the ball is dropping toward you, lean backward. Raise up on your toes and draw in your stomach to soften the impact. The ball will bounce only a few inches before dropping to your feet. If the ball comes in at a lower angle, lean over the ball to guide it down to your feet. Withdraw your chest at impact to deaden the shot.

It is important to keep your arms clear when trapping with the chest because any contact with any part of the arm will cause loss of the ball and a direct-kick penalty.

HEADING

Beginners may be a little fearful of the ball. They wonder if it's going to hurt. If done correctly, heading shouldn't hurt.

The most difficult thing about heading is the natural tendency to close your eyes as the ball comes near your head. You must try to keep your eyes open and look at the ball in flight. Strike the ball — don't let it strike you. Coaches will often start beginners with a deflated soccer ball, or use a volley-ball, for softer contact with the head until the player becomes experienced and gains confidence.

A word of caution: never attempt to head a ball coming at you below the chest line. If you drop your head lower than your chest, you stand a chance of being kicked in the head.

A popular exercise used by coaches to train beginners in ball control with the head is to have you use your head to keep the ball airborne about 12 to 18 inches above your head. This helps develop a sense of touch vital to good ball control.

The body plays an important role in basic heading technique. Heading requires that you coordinate your feet, legs, trunk and neck for timing and direction. Your feet and legs form the power base for heading the ball. When you head the ball you should have the upper part of your body bent backwards. Your knees should be bent slightly as well. Swing forward with your trunk as your forehead strikes the ball. Straighten your knees after contact to add force. It is important that you don't just let the ball drop onto your head; you must punch the ball as powerfully as possible.

Besides heading the ball forward from a standing position, you should learn to head the ball while on the run and while jumping. **A jumping header provides more power than a standing header. Timing is vital. You can jump with one leg or both. Using your arms to keep your balance, jump as high as possible.** If feasible, take a short run before you leap. Learn to jump with either leg because you won't always have a choice in actual play.

Many times, a heading play will call for a certain direction: downwards while aiming for the goal, sideways or backwards to pass. Upward headers are usually done when defending.

You can change the direction of an incoming ball by turning your trunk, neck and head at contact with the ball, using your forehead to strike the ball in the intended direction. **For a downward header, your forehead must strike directly behind the ball and above the middle of it. Tuck your chin in and move your trunk forward and toward the ground. An upward header is accomplished by striking from beneath the ball with a powerful jump.**

TACKLING

Tackling in soccer means taking the ball away from your opponent by using your feet. Tackling can also mean forcing your opponent to kick the ball out of bounds and thus give your team possession of the ball. Or it can serve as a blocking maneuver that forces your foe to make a bad pass. Developing tackling skills is important to good defensive play. A tackler must be careful not to trip the player, which is a rule violation. Yet you must get close to your opponent to be effective. Alertness, timing, and swift movement are essential. Do not lunge for the ball. You must be in a balanced position so you can make a quick move for the ball.

Tackling can be done from the front, side, or rear. Although you can't push with your hands or elbows, you are permitted to block the player with your shoulders. You cannot charge violently with your shoulders, or you will be penalized. And shoulder charging is only legal when shoulder hits shoulder. A shoulder charge is best executed when you are running alongside your opponent, so you can attempt to knock the player off the ball.

To make a front tackle, you must first block the ball with one foot and then quickly kick it away with the other foot. It's best to use the inside of either foot as it is the most effective trapping area. Lift your foot up with your ankle in a rigid position, to better take the impact against the ball. You can avoid being pushed off balance if you crouch forward. Spread your legs far enough for good balance, but not so far apart that the opponent can slip the ball between them.

There will be times in defensive situations when the most effective method of stopping an opponent is to use a sliding tackle. Here the objective is not so much to gain possession of the ball but to kick it away from the attacker. Timing is essential because you will risk missing the ball and possibly tripping the player which is a foul (there is no foul if you kick the ball away before contact with the opponent). Try to kick the ball to a teammate, if possible, or out of bounds. The kick must be solid or the attacker can regain possession of the ball.

Sometimes you may find yourself in a position to use a heel tackle, a more advanced skill. The ideal situation is when the attacker and defender are running shoulder to shoulder in the same direction, and particularly if the defender is on the same side as the attacker's dribbling leg. Here, again, good timing is important. You must time your stride with that of the attacker and, at the precise moment, move your inside leg into the path of the ball and block it with your heel. Since this causes the ball to reverse its direction, you must pivot quickly to reverse your run into the direction of the ball.

RUNNING

Soccer players spend much of their time running as they maneuver to get into position to shoot, pass or to defend. Running is also done when you have possession of the ball in the clear and close dribbling is not needed. You then push the ball a greater distance ahead and run at a faster speed after it. Control of the ball while running is easier if you turn in your toes so that the ball is tapped with the outside of the foot. Take shorter steps for better ball control, and be able to quickly reverse your direction when necessary. Look ahead of the ball as much as possible so you can watch your opponent's moves. A good player also does a lot of running when a teammate is dribbling with the ball because it is important to get into a position to receive a pass.

THROWING-IN

The only time a player, other than a goalkeeper, can get his hands on the ball is on a throw-in. All players should learn to do it effectively so that there's no likelihood of losing possession of the ball because of a bad throw-in.

The rules state that both hands must be on the ball while delivering it for the throw-in and the player must face the field of play, and part of each foot should be either on the touchline or on the ground outside the touchline. The ball must be delivered from behind and over the head. The thrower may not play the ball until it has been touched by another player.

There are three styles of throw-in: feet together, feet approximately shoulder width apart, or one foot in front of the other. The throw-in is a comparatively easy play to accomplish. Hold the ball in both hands with your fingers spread comfortably apart on both sides of the ball and slightly to the rear of the ball. Spreading the feet apart provides the best balance. As you prepare to throw, place the ball well behind your head and flex your knees forward in the direction of the throw. Lean your trunk backward (just how much is determined by the distance you are throwing). This cocking of the body is followed by the throwing action with the knees straightening and the body moving forward and the arms whipping the ball as they come over and through. Some players prefer to have one foot in front of the other so that they can achieve greater power by shifting the weight from the rear leg to the front leg. Both feet must remain on the ground. A short run will also provide greater power and distance, but both feet must still be on the ground at the time of delivery. A running throw-in is best performed with one foot in front of the other. Begin your throw well away from the line as you need space to stop to avoid going over the line.

PASSING

Soccer is a passing game, and no player or team can be successful without doing it well.

When you see a team with sparkling offensive play, you will always see players making fast and accurate passes. Passes can be short or long and they can delivered with your foot, leg, chest, head or any part of your body except your arms and hands.

Good passing requires that you deliver the ball to a teammate at the right moment — when the receiver can properly make the next move. You must be able to anticipate the receiver's moves, and you can do this best if you develop the technique of taking your eyes off the ball while you are controlling it.

Various kicking methods can be employed for passing. An inside-of-the-foot kick is used for most passes but an outside-of-the-foot kick is good for short passes. A volley kick, using the inside of your foot, is used when the ball comes to you in the air. Instep kicks provide distance for long passes. A backward pass can be made by using the sole of your foot by placing your foot on the ball to stop it and then rolling it backward. The heel of the foot can also be effective in making a short backward pass. A good player also learns how to pass using the head and chest.

Skillful passing is accomplished by a lot of practice. Experienced coaches will usually require more passing practice drills than any other phase of the game. Rigid practice sessions can help players learn how to move the ball fast and accurately. Drills will enable players to develop their timing so they can lead the receiver with the ball without the receiver breaking stride. Players will learn just how far to lead other teammates on a pass, as they learn each other's abilities.

Effective passing involves being able to surprise your opponents by mixing the types of passes and faking the direction of the pass (such as passing it in the opposite direction from which you are running). You can't always use short ground passes because they are the safest; your opponents will soon learn to anticipate it.

SCREENING

Screening is the art of ball control by using your body to keep an opponent away from the ball. Naturally, the farther away you can keep the defender from the ball the better your chance of controlling it. Always try to control the ball with the foot farthest away from the opponent. Turn your body so that you are between the defender and the ball.

SHOOTING

Of course, getting a shot on goal is one of the most exciting moments in soccer. **Look at the target before you start your kick because once your kicking swing begins, you must keep your eyes on the ball.** Try to keep your shots low and aim for the corners of the goal. Instep and outside-of-the-foot kicks are best for ground balls. Half volley shots are used for higher shots, while a header does the job when the ball comes to you higher than your chest.

A goalkeeper's ready position requires good balance for mobility.

CHAPTER FIVE • POSITIONS: HOW TO PLAY THEM

Soccer is played with 11 players to a team: five forwards, three halfbacks, two fullbacks, and one goalkeeper. Because the ball constantly changes possession from one team to the other and action is fast, all players must be able to move quickly and handle both an offensive or defensive play. Let's have a look at the duties of each of the various positions. Players should understand the function of each position so that team play can be more easily coordinated.

GOALKEEPER

Goalkeepers need a different set of skills than the other positions. They are specialists in defense. The goal-keepers work alone and the position calls for a wide variety of skills: speed, agility, good hands, jumping and kicking ability, good eyes, excellent concentration and coordination, and courage. The goal-keeper is the only player in soccer who is permitted to use the hands. They have the tough — and exciting — task of protecting a goal which is 24 feet wide and eight feet high.

Goalkeeping demands that the "goalie" keep the eyes on the ball at all times, the body between the goal and the ball, and catch and stop the ball whenever possible. Goalies must learn how to set up the proper position to reduce the shooter's angle on the goal. When gaining possession of the ball, the goalie starts the team's offensive attack, either by kicking the ball or throwing it to a teammate.

Goalies are required to stop a variety of shots and each demands a technique all its own. **For ground balls, the best method is to get down on one knee so that your hands are backed up by your legs.** Most of your weight should be on your non-kneeling leg so you can move quickly if the ball takes an unexpected bounce. **The ball should then be quickly pulled up to your chest for protection against a collision with an opponent.**

To catch balls coming to you chest-high move your body in front of the ball and hold your arms up in front with the elbows close to the sides. Let your arms "give" toward your body as you catch the ball, cushioning the impact. On catching it, bend your body over the ball for better protection.

In catching high balls, face the direction of the ball's flight. Keep your eyes on the ball as you make your move. Raise one knee as protection against opponents who may run into you. Soon as you catch the ball, draw it to your chest area and protect it with the arms.

Balls coming at you too high or too fast to catch should be **punched and deflected away.** You can punch the ball away by using both fists clenched side by side. High balls can also be deflected over the bar or around the goal post.

There will be times when diving will be the only way to stop the ball. The ball can either be caught or fisted away from the goal. The objective is to get your hand into position to protect the lower corner of the goal. The arm at the side of the approaching ball is thrust at the ball, while the legs push off keeping the body low to the ground. As soon as the stop is made, both hands should pull the ball into the body for better protection.

Goalkeepers should never attempt to kick the ball while in a defensive play as it would be a dangerous move that could result in the ball bouncing or deflecting from your foot into the goal.

As a goalkeeper, once you have possession of the ball you must get rid of it quickly to begin your team's offensive attack. You do this by throwing the ball or kicking it to a teammate upfield.

The safest way to get a ball to a teammate is usually by throwing the ball since it is easier to achieve accuracy with a toss than a kick. **For a long pass, use an overhand throw, similar to that used by baseball players.** The throw must be quick and powerful so that opponents don't have much time to set up a defense.

An underhand throwing motion, similar to bowling, is a good method of getting a short pass to a teammate on the ground, allowing the player to move on it immediately.

While punting the ball upfield can make it go high and far, it is usually not as effective as throwing the ball. Often defenders can get to the punted ball as easily as your teammates. The punt is best made when you cannot spot a teammate to throw to. Use an instep kick and punt the ball like a football player.

Under the rules, a goalie cannot carry the ball more than four steps before releasing it. If carried five or more steps, an indirect free kick is awarded to your opponents.

When an opponent breaks through alone and is heading toward the goal, the goalie often will come out of the goal so as to narrow the angle, creating less of a target and forcing the player to shoot from farther out.

Studying your opponents' shooting style of play and learning which foot they favor for kicking will prove quite helpful in planning your defensive tactics.

It is important that you learn where to stand so the least amount of target is offered. Stand on the left side of the goal for all attacks coming from your left; stand a few feet from the left goal post. Do the opposite if the attack is from your right. Stand in the center of the goal for an attack coming straight on. You need to take a well-balanced stance so you can move in either direction. Flex your knees slightly so you can spring into action.

FORWARDS

There are five forwards in soccer, a center forward and two inside and outside forwards. They are commonly referred to as "strikers." Outside forwards are also referred to as "wingers" or "wings." Whatever they're called, they are the team's major attack force and, being such, they must be talented in kicking, passing, dribbling, heading, and trapping. They must be accurate shooters, and they must know how to feint their moves to confuse the opponents.

Being in the middle of the action, the center forward gets the most opportunities to score. Chances to score come quickly; so, the center forward must be able to shoot fast and accurately. Being able to shoot well with both feet is a major asset for a center forward. The position also demands good heading techniques. Center forwards are usually taller or more rugged players because they must perform in the closely guarded penalty area where there is a lot of body contact. The position also calls for the center forward to be able to pass quickly and accurately and be an expert dribbler. Because of close guarding the center forward often serves as a decoy to lure defensive players out of position, making an opening for an inside forward to move with the ball.

Inside forwards have the responsibility of setting up plays. They must have speed and be good passers and shooters. Since they often go downfield to assist defense, they rove and cover more ground than other players. Endurance is a prime requirement. Inside forwards control the midfield area, breaking up the opponents' attacks to gain possession of the ball and develop an offensive play. Inside forwards work closely with the halfbacks to control the midfield area. When not in possession of the ball, inside forwards move back toward their defensive area. They must also defend against corner kicks when playing defense.

Outside forwards, "wings" or "wingers," patrol the touchlines on their sides. They, too, must possess speed and be very good at ball control. **They should be fast dribblers, quick and accurate with passes, and able to trap effectively.** Outside forwards are often selected by the goalkeeper after making a save, to receive passes; they also receive them on throw-ins. **Thus, outside forwards initiate offensive attacks.** They have to be able to shoot quickly and accurately. Outside forwards assist halfbacks and fullbacks on their side of the field in defensive play.

HALFBACKS

The three halfbacks, or midfieldmen as they are usually called today, are primarily concerned with defense and they are also the ones who link a team's offense. These duties call for a lot of running, so stamina is an important factor.

Possession of the ball changes constantly at midfield, so halfbacks must be able to act quickly in either a defensive or offensive play. They must be good tacklers. Ability to anticipate the other players' moves is a definite asset.

Halfbacks must pass accurately because when they gain possession of the ball they send it on to forwards as they attack the goal. Halfbacks also receive passes from forwards as they move up behind them in an offensive action, and then they can return a pass to a forward in good scoring position.

A halfback, usually an outside or wing player, may penetrate deep into enemy territory to support an attack of a forward teammate. The other outside back will stay behind to support the defense.

The center halfback, stationed between the two outside halfbacks, has the responsibility of covering the opposing center forward. The center halfback must be able to move quickly and trap, tackle and kick effectively under the pressure of heavy action. Center halfbacks play a vital role in offense, too, as they are often firing passes to outside halfbacks and forwards after gaining possession of the ball in defensive play. Accuracy and quickness is essential for the passes to find their mark.

Due to the strategic location, the center halfback position calls for a player who can handle the responsibilities of being a central figure on both defense and offense. Taller players are usually preferred for this position, but regardless of size, the center halfback must be good at leaping high in the air and heading the ball.

FULLBACKS

There are two fullbacks, known as defenders, and they must be strong tacklers as their major responsibilities are defensive. **Fullbacks form the heart of the defense and it's their duty to protect the goal and the goalkeeper from attacks.** They must be talented kickers and headers, able to clear the ball away quickly. A fullback who can kick great distances is quite valuable to the team, but the kicks should be aimed at a teammate who is in the open.

Fullbacks must be adept at anticipating moves by attackers so they can act quickly. They should be strong tacklers and good at tight guarding of opponents. Fullbacks rarely have an opportunity to dribble the ball as their duties keep them deep inside their own territory. But, when in possession of the ball and in the open, the fullback can dribble to midfield to initiate the team's attack, seeking to pass to a forward. When this play occurs, halfbacks cover the fullback's vacated position.

Fullbacks try to force opponents to the sidelines whenever possible so that the player's target area on the goal is greatly reduced.

A fullback who is forced to face two forwards working together must not go for the ball, but drop back to keep the body between the ball and the goal. The fullback must keep an alert eye on the player who doesn't have the ball as the dribbler may make a pass. Whenever a goalkeeper leaves the goal area in pursuit of the ball, a fullback must move into the goal to cover it.

CHAPTER SIX ● TEAM PLAY

Soccer, unlike football which has offensive and defensive players, requires that all players be capable of performing both offense and defense. The constant quick-changing ball possession means that a player on the attack may suddenly have to switch to defensive play.

No matter how good the eleven individual players, if each is playing only for one's self, they are of poor value to the team. Any successful soccer team is one that functions as a unit — each player contributing his or her own skills to plays that will do the team the most good. This produces goals, and that's how games are won. The players must operate as a *whole* team to function effectively, both on offense and defense.

In football, there's an old saying "the best defense is a good offense." This can hold true to some extent in soccer, too, but the difference is that the ball changes hands more frequently. Naturally, the more a team has possession of the ball, the less it is defending. But, in soccer, it is also true that the team which is better at defense will gain possession of the ball more often. Therefore, each player must perform his or her best both on offense and defense and operate as a team to be successful. A player who shines on offense but neglects defensive play is not a good team player.

Each player has the responsibility of staying in good physical condition. Soccer demands speed, alertness and stamina. An out-of-condition player not only will tire too soon but is also apt to get injured.

OFFENSE

Soccer teams use various formations, the style chosen is usually based on the abilities of the players and the strengths and weaknesses of the opposition. Coaches who know the playing characteristics of their opponents can determine a playing style that will be better prepared to cope with the enemy's strengths and take advantage of their weaknesses.

Regardless of the system used, the objective is to penetrate into the opponents' defense and get to the goal. **The attacking team, to be most effective, must operate across the width of the field, from touchline to touchline. Wings will move down the sidelines with the ball while other forwards seek better field positions to receive passes.**

A popular formation in recent years has been the 4-3-3. Four backs as defenders, three midfielders, and three forwards as strikers. This formation, if the three midfielders are strong, mobile players, provides a good balance for offensive and defensive moves.

Another widely used basic formation is called the "W", which uses the center and outside forwards as the major attackers with the two inside forwards playing farther back so from the air the five players form the shape of a "W." If the team emphasizes long passes, it will use a deep W formation with the inside forwards playing well back.

Soccer is a game that calls for a lot of passing, and that means a team's offense is usually only as good as its passing. The attacking team should be very mobile, continually moving and searching for unguarded open spaces to receive passes. Besides penetrating the defense down the sidelines, a team should use considerable cross-passing across the complete width of the field. Passes that surprise opponents are usually most successful so there has to be a variety of passes. Long passes. Short passes. High passes. Ground passes. Passing the ball in the opposite direction from which you are running.

A decoy pass is one method of surprising the opponents. One, two or three players run past the teammate in possession of the ball and call for a pass, but then another teammate moves up and unexpectedly receives the pass.

To be most effective in offensive play, a team needs depth in its attack. This calls for players without the ball to move into the opponents' defense in search of good receiving positions to give the teammate with the ball more opportunities to pass.

Attacks are more effective if the attackers advance one behind another rather than in a straight line across the field. The idea is to force the opponents to defend each player individually instead of allowing one defender to move between the passer and the receiver and being able to cover both players.

A strong offense requires talented strikers, players good at dribbling, screening and passing and heading. They must be alert and able to move quickly, and capable of turning with the ball both to the right and left.

A team can present a much more formidable offense if it is strongly drilled in playing direct or indirect free kicks, corner kicks, goal kicks, penalty kicks and sideline kicks. Good practice sessions on those kicking plays will pay off with more goals.

DEFENSE

Whenever a soccer team loses possession of the ball, the team is on defense — and that means every player must be prepared to defend and tackle, regardless of his or her position.

Soccer teams use two basic defensive plans: the player-to-player method and zone defense, or both systems in combination. In the player-to-player defense, each defensive player covers a particular attacking player. For example, the two fullbacks can cover the opponents' outside forwards, while the center halfback guards the enemy's center forward, with the halfbacks watching the opposing inside forwards.

How far a defensive player keeps from an opponent is determined by the enemy's location on the field; if the foe gets near the penalty area with the ball, the defensive player moves in close. Otherwise, it's usually about three or four yards away. Of course, if an opponent is exceptionally fast, it is better to move in closer.

When each defensive player is in charge of a particular area of the field and must cover any attacker entering that area it is called the zone defense. Zone defense is useful when the attacking team has a mobile style of play where the forwards constantly interchange positions. Sometimes, a team will only use a zone defense when the ball is upfield, and will switch to a player-to-player defense when the ball moves to the penalty area.

Bunching up in defense in the penalty area is a good way to stop an attack and gain possession of the ball.

Both the player-to-player and zone defense systems have a basic weakness. In the former, there's a hole every time a defender is beaten; in the latter, the disadvantage is a greater amount of space available to opponents. These problems can be solved, however, by employing a free player as a "sweeper" behind or in front of the defensive line: the sweeper challenges the player with the ball while teammates stay with the assigned area or opponent.

Defense tactics call for different techniques, depending upon the play. Under certain situations the defender strives to use a good tackle to take the ball away from an opponent in possession. Other times, the defender will cause the player with the ball to get rid of it hurriedly and make a poor pass. An attempt will be made by the defender to intercept a pass intended for a player that he or she is guarding. Sometimes all that is possible is to prevent a potential receiver from getting a pass.

It is important that defensive players be prepared to interchange defense duties with teammates. If an attacking player gets past a defensive opponent such as a halfback, then a fullback has to move up quickly to cover.

Each area of the playing field presents a different challenge and technique for the defender. Tackling a player along the sidelines is not as difficult as doing it at midfield where an opponent has more room to maneuver.

Teams will almost always concentrate several players in the penalty area to stop passes and shots or dribbling through. Bunching up in defense in the penalty area is a good way to stop an attack and gain possession of the ball.

Care and good judgement must be exercised in attempting any tackling at midfield. If you miss your tackle, you are left behind at midfield and your opponents will outnumber your team as they head toward the penalty area. Oftentimes, it's best to run with your opponent and retreat back to your main line of defense for more strength in defense. A retreating defense is a common method in use today because it gives the defending team a chance to organize for greater depth.

* *

No soccer team is going to be successful without a good program of physical conditioning for its players. Strength, speed and endurance are developed through a steady training schedule, which can include running laps around the field, short sprints, ball gymnastics, calisthenics, and a practice game between team members. It is up to each player to take care of his or her body, to eat nutritious food, get enough hours of sleep and avoid unhealthy habits.

Soccer is a great sport for conditioning the body. And, in playing it, you will have fun, learn sportsmanship and make friends.

ABOUT THE AUTHOR

Jack Scagnetti is the author of 11 books, five of them on sports subjects. A former newspaper sports writer in suburban Detroit, he also served for eight years as public relations director and business manager for a private athletic club in Detroit which sponsored teams in every major sport, including youth soccer. Scagnetti has authored more than 800 national magazine articles, many of them on sports. A free-lance writer since 1968, he makes his home in North Hollywood, California.